Play through the Bible

Alice Buckley

Design and illustration by André Parker
Edited by Alison Mitchell

Play on the Word
©Alice Buckley/The Good Book Company, 2014

Published by The Good Book Company
Tel (UK): 0333 123 0880, International: +44 (0) 208 942 0880 Email: info@thegoodbook.co.uk
UK: www.thegoodbook.co.uk North America: www.thegoodbook.com
Australia: www.thegoodbook.com.au New Zealand: www.thegoodbook.co.nz

Additional photography ©istockphoto.com ISBN: 978190959196 Printed by Proost Industries NV, Belgium

Contents

Welcome!

Life with pre-schoolers is exhausting. It's lovely, and funny, and brilliant too, but *oh*, it's exhausting!

We're trying to teach them to count to five, teach them to use the potty, teach them to *please* stop drawing on their hands. Sometimes teaching our kids about Jesus feels like one more thing on a never-ending list.

I wrote this book for tired, busy parents.

I wrote this book for parents who want their kids to know Jesus but find it hard to teach them about him.

I wrote this book for parents who know it's their job to introduce their children to Jesus but have no idea where to start.

I wrote this book for parents who want new ideas for their family Bible times or want something that complements what they are already doing.

In this book you will find 20 stories about Jesus with simple words and easy suggestions for making storytime memorable for your whole family.

There are also lots of play ideas to help reinforce the message of the story, offer natural opportunities to talk about Jesus, and above all *have fun as you get to know Jesus.*

Alice

How to use this book...

It's brilliant to be able to read the Bible with our children. Each family will do this is in very different ways, but there are some things that work for nearly everyone.

When you have your Bible-reading time, try doing it at the same time of day in the same place. Setting up a routine like this really helps little ones.

Try to do a Bible time regularly. For some families this means doing it every day—for others it might mean reading together at the weekends.

We're introducing our children to our good and gracious God. Let's agree not to guilt-trip when we miss a day (or week, or month!), or when our Bible time is a disaster because one child had a tantrum, another needed a wee and the baby cried so loudly no one could hear anyway. Deal?

Story

A short and simple story based on a passage from the Gospel of Luke. Try doing actions for the words in bold or use some of the other storytelling ideas. Read this story with your child every day for a week.

Prayer

A short prayer to help you and your child respond to the story.

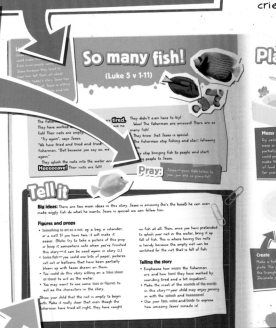

Tell it

Suggestions of figures, props and ways of telling the story that will help engage and involve your child and make the story come to life.

Play it

At least six ideas (on the page, plus more online) based on the big themes in the story. These are designed to help you and your child get to know the story better, and to have fun as you chat and discover more about Jesus.

Tips

It's a good idea for you to have read the passage the **story** is based on in your own Bible. Not every bit of the Gospel of Luke is covered in the stories so it's well worth reading the bits we miss out too!

Tip

Some parents encourage their children to close their eyes or put their hands together when they pray, and others are happy for their kids to be more wriggly. It's entirely up to you! Your child can join in by saying "Amen" at the end or by repeating the words after you.

Throughout this book I've suggested ways to tell each story that will help capture your child's imagination and attention. Pick and choose from the ideas, and encourage your child to join in too. You don't have to do it all!

Our storytelling suggestions are split into two sections: **figures and props,** and **telling the story.** Each is a different method of telling the story in an engaging way, which will help your child to join in too.

Figures and props: These are a favourite in our family! Our children love it when we use objects and illustrations to help tell our stories. I've given you ideas for each story. These really help focus attention and encourage our children to be hands-on.

Telling the story: You don't need me to tell you how to read a story with expression and pace! You do it every time you read to your child (except maybe when it's the fifteenth reading of the same book!). But I've included some suggestions for how you can use your body and voice to add interest and include your child as you tell the story.

Actions: Actions are an amazing way of helping little ones express themselves even when their speech hasn't quite caught up with their understanding! Actions are really fun for older children too. You'll notice each story has some words in **bold** —these are words that lend themselves to being acted out. You can either make up your own actions or look at my suggestions on page 54.

In our family we tend to do a little bit of each method—we have a prop or two, choose a couple of actions, and attempt to tell the story in an interesting and expressive way. There isn't one right way to tell these stories—the right way is whatever suits your family best!

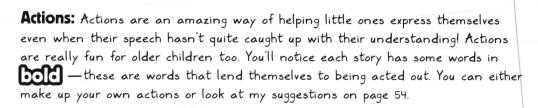

Play themes: This is a list of the themes a week's play ideas have been based on. The **play themes** reinforce the **"big ideas"** and help to remind your child of the story as you play. Feel free to use your own play ideas as well!

Select ideas from the play suggestions which suit your child's age, stage and interests, and that fit easily into your routine.

Tip Use the play ideas and repeated words from the story to prompt natural conversation about Jesus through the week.

Here comes Jesus
(Luke 3 v 15-22)

Story:

God's people have been waiting.

They have been waiting for God's **King** to come.

God's people have been waiting... and waiting... and WAITING for God's Son, the **King,** to come to the rescue.

When John comes, the people say:

"Are you God's Son? Are you God's **King!"**

"No!" says John. "Wait! God's Son, the **King,** is coming soon. Get ready for him!"

When Jesus comes, the people hear God say:

"Yes! You are my Son! I love you! I am so pleased with you!"

Hooray! The **King** is here! God's Son Jesus— **God to the rescue!**

Pray:
Thank you God that Jesus came to the rescue!

Tell it

Big idea: Jesus is God's Son—the King the people have been waiting for.

Figures and props

- **A figure or toy** to act as John.
- **A figure or toy** to act as Jesus.

Have John on show and Jesus somewhere close so that you can bring him out as you tell the story.

When you talk about John, point to the figure you are using to act as him.

When you talk about Jesus coming, bring in your Jesus figure and draw your child's attention to him.

Telling the story

- **Waiting** is a big theme of this story. Emphasise the idea of waiting by **sighing, snoring** or doing your best **"tired and bored"** face!
- The tone of the story changes as you read it—from **slow** and rather **weary** at the beginning to **excited** and **happy** at the end—so reflect that in your voice and facial expressions as you tell it.

Play it

"Heeeelp!"

Create

Make a book together by printing off colouring sheets of your child's favourite book or TV characters from online. Decorate them and make them into a book using a ring binder or stapler. Finish your book with a picture of your child.

Read the book together asking: "Is that my son/daughter?!" on each page. When you reach the picture of your child say: "Yes! That's my son/daughter! I love you!".

Out and about

Be superheroes in the park or garden, or as you walk to the shops. Pretend to be in trouble and get your child to come to the rescue.

Other ideas...

Messy

Prepare food together. Choose something that requires your child to wait as it cooks or cools. While you are waiting, spend time getting ready to eat. For example: wash hands, get a plate, clear space on the table. Remind your child of the waiting and getting ready in the story.

Pretend

Play at being kings (or queens, or any other person your child will think is very special). Imagine you are getting ready for a special visitor. What will you do to get ready? How does it feel to wait?

Active

Use games of hide and seek. Remind your child of the story by using the words "wait" and "get ready!" a lot while you play.

Playing anyway

Find photos of families your child knows and play a game matching the children to the parents.

For loads more ideas of how to "Play it", go to

www. thegoodbook .com/playit

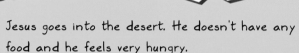

Jesus in the desert
(Luke 4 v 1-13)

Story:

Jesus goes into the desert. He doesn't have any food and he feels very hungry.

The devil comes to Jesus. (The devil tries to stop people **listening** to God.)

"Listen" to me!" says the devil. "I can help you get food."

"Listen" to me!" says the devil. "If you're God's Son, turn these stones into bread."

"Listen" to me!" says the devil. "Do what I say, then you won't be hungry."

"No!" says Jesus. "I won't **listen** to you. I will **listen** to God."

Jesus is God's Son. He always **listens** to God and does what he says.

Pray:

Thank you Jesus—you always listened to God. Please help me to listen to you and do what you say.

Tell it

Big idea: Jesus is God's Son—he always listens to God and does what he says.

Figures and props

- **Sand or table salt** to act as the desert.
- **An empty dish and spoon**—have enough of both so your child can join in too.
- **Some stones.** (or bits of crumpled paper instead).

Let your child touch the sand when you talk about the desert.

When you talk about Jesus having no food, pretend to eat from your bowl but gasp with dismay when you see there is nothing to eat.

Pick up the stones when the devil tells Jesus to turn them into bread. Allow your child to hold and touch the stones too.

Telling the story

- **Listening** is a big theme in this story so accentuate the word **"listen"** as you say it.

Tip

You can mix and match ideas from "Play it". Don't try to do too many things at once. Being too simple is always better than being too complicated!

Play it

Messy

Play with sand or table salt in a baking dish. Pretend to be in a desert. Hide stones in the sand and see if your child can find theml. (Rubbing sandy hands with baby powder helps get sand off skin easily.) Chat together about the story.

Out and about

Do a listening scavenger hunt while out for a walk or in the garden. Ask your child to listen while you tell them something to find. Then they must bring you the item or stand next to it. (For example: a leaf, a stone, a red door, a street light.)

Other ideas...

Pretend

Play with toy animals. Pretend to be a father or mother animal and make its noise. See if your child can find the animal that matches the noise. Celebrate when the animal has listened to its mother or father.

Active

Do games that involve listening and doing, such as "Simon says".

Playing anyway

Our children don't always listen and do what we say perfectly like Jesus did! When this happens, it's a great chance to talk about how amazing Jesus is and how different he is from us.

Create

Can you make bread out of stones?! Put some stones in a bowl and give them a mix. Talk about how we can't make bread that way!

For loads more ideas of how to "Play it", go to

www.thegoodbook.com/playit

Jesus makes lots of people better

(Luke 4 v 40-44)

Story:

It's getting dark. Is it time for bed?

Jesus is too busy to go to bed. There are lots of people with him—people who are ill and people who are hurt.

Can Jesus make them better?

Will Jesus use a bandage to make them better? **No!**

Will Jesus use medicine to make them better? **No!**

What do you think he will use? He uses his **hands!**

Jesus the ill people and right away, just like that, they are totally and completely better!

Wow, Jesus—you're amazing!

Pray:

Wow Jesus, you made people better just by touching them—you're amazing!

Tell it

Big idea: Jesus can make people better by touching them—he must be very powerful and special.

Figures and props

- **Figures or toys** to act as ill people (try to take a picture of the bandaged-up toys, or keep them somewhere safe when you've finished, to use again in the story on page 34).
- **Bandages** (or strips of toilet tissue!).
- **Medicine spoons** or **dosing syringes**

Use your props on the toys as you tell the story. When you talk about Jesus healing people, stand your toys up and get them to move around as though they are well.

Telling the story

- When you ask questions in this story, look **puzzled**: shrug your shoulders, scratch your head and say **"hmmm"**! Pause to make time for your child to respond to the question (**"no!"**) if they want to.
- It's **amazing** that Jesus can make people better just by **touching** them! As you tell the story, use your **voice** and your **face** to show how **surprising** and **wonderful** it is.

Tip Keeping the way you tell the story the same for the whole week can help your child get to know it well and feel confident about joining in.

Play it

Create

Make handprint pictures and talk about Jesus making people better just by touching them with his hands.

Pretend

Play at being doctors. Or be paramedics and zoom around rescuing people who are hurt and ill.

Other ideas...

RIIIIIIP!

Out and about

Visit your nearest drugstore or pharmacy. Look at all the different things there are to make people feel better. Take a basket and ask your child to put in the things Jesus would need to use. Make it very funny: "Does Jesus need antiseptic cream?" No! "Does he need bandages?" No! "Does he need hair dye?" No!!

Chat and play

Talk about times your child has felt ill or been hurt. How did they get better? If they have visited a doctor or hospital, talk about the things that were used to help them.

Playing anyway

When your child has a bump while they're playing, offer to make it better just by touching it. Show them that you can't do it!

Messy

Find some broken things and see what your child can mend with their hands. For example: broken cookies, broken LEGO towers, a torn page of a book, a toy with a piece removed which can be replaced.

For loads more ideas of how to "Play it", go to

www.thegoodbook.com/playit

Link: Lots of people came to Jesus because they knew he could make them feel better. Even more people came to Jesus because they loved to hear him tell them all about God! In today's story Jesus has borrowed a boat. Jesus is sitting in the boat telling lots and lots of people all about God.

So many fish!
(Luke 5 v 1-11)

Story:

The fishermen in the boat with Jesus are **tired.** They have worked all night long but they have no fish! Their nets are empty.

"Try again," says Jesus.

"We have tried and tried and tried!" say the fishermen. "But because you say so, we will try again."

They splosh the nets into the water and…

He-e-e-e-eave! Their nets are full!

They didn't even have to try!

Wow! The fishermen are amazed! There are so many fish!

They know that Jesus is special.

The fishermen stop fishing and start following Jesus.

They stop bringing fish to people and start bringing people to Jesus.

Pray:
Jesus—even fish listen to you, you are so powerful!

Tell it

Big ideas: There are two main ideas in this story. Jesus is amazing (he's the boss!): he can even make wiggly fish do what he wants. Jesus is special: we can follow him.

Figures and props

- **Something to act as a net,** eg: a bag, a colander, or a net! If you have two, it will make it easier. (Note: Try to take a picture of this prop or keep it somewhere safe when you've finished this story—it can be used again on page 34.)
- **Some fish**—you could use bits of paper, pictures cut out or balloons that have been partially blown up with faces drawn on them.
- You could do this story sitting on a **blue sheet or towel** to act as the water.
- You may want to use some **toys or figures** to act as the characters in the story.

Show your child that the net is empty to begin with. Make it really clear that even though the fishermen have tried all night, they have caught no fish at all. Then, once you have pretended to splosh your net in the water, bring it up full of fish. This is where having two nets is handy because the empty net can be switched for the net that is full of fish.

Telling the story

- Emphasise how **weary** the fishermen are and how **hard** they have worked by sounding tired and a bit impatient.
- Make the most of the **sounds of the words** in this story—your child may enjoy joining in with the **splosh** and **he-e-e-e-eave!**
- Use your **face, voice** and **body** to express how **amazing** Jesus' miracle is!

Play it

Messy

Try catching fish in the bath. Use a colander, sieve or tea-strainer as a net and try using partially inflated balloons as fish to catch. You could put a drop of food colouring in the bath to make the water blue or green. A couple of drops of food colouring shouldn't stain your bathtub (or your child!).

Pretend

Pretend to be in a fishing boat (on the sofa or sat on cushions on the floor). Place toys on the floor around your child and see what they can catch. Use a bag or tub as a net (an old ice-cream or margarine tub would work well).

Other ideas...

Out and about

Visit a pet shop that sells fish, or go and see a friend who has pet fish. Try to tell the fish what to do and where to swim.

Active

Blow bubbles and get your child to try to catch them. Remind them of the story and how hard it was for the fishermen to catch anything without Jesus.

Chat and play

Use words from the story as you chat and play this week, like "tried and tried" and "empty" and "full". Eat fish this week and talk about the story.

Create

Make a fish by cutting a triangle out of a paper plate. The gap that is left is the mouth. Stick the triangle on the opposite edge to be a tail. Decorate your fish and hang it on string.

For loads more ideas of how to "Play it", go to

www.thegoodbook.com/playit

15

Link: More and more people hear about the amazing things Jesus can do. They've never met anyone like him!

Jesus helps a man who can't walk

(Luke 5 v 17-26)

Story:

Here is a man who can't **walk.**
His friends carry him on a mat.
One busy day they go and see Jesus.
Jesus knows just what the man needs. "I forgive you. You can be **friends** with God!"
Jesus knows just what the man wants. "I can help you. Get up and **walk!"**

The man **walks** away feeling very happy!
He is **friends** with God.

Hooray!

Pray:

Thank you God for my friends. Thank you that you want us to be your friends.

Tell it

Big idea: Jesus can do amazing things—he can even make us God's friends.

Figures and props

- **A figure or toy** to act as the man.
- **A figure or toy** to act as Jesus.
- **Some toys or figures** to act as the friends.

To begin the story, show your child the man lying down being helped by his friends. Show the friends taking the man to Jesus. At the end of the story, show that the man has gone from lying down to standing up and walking about.

Telling the story

- End the story with **excitement** and **enthusiasm**—encourage your child to show a **happy** face and **cheer!**

Tip

This is a short story so your child can get to know it really well. Encourage your child to join in with the words and actions. Ask your child to tell you the story at the end of the week!

Play it

Messy

Fill a plastic bottle with half cooking oil and half coloured water. Add a squirt of dish soap and some glitter. Fasten the bottle well and watch out for your child attempting to unscrew the lid! When the bottle is shaken the two parts seem to blend, but end up separate again. Use this to talk about forgiveness and being friends with God.

Create

Help your child make a chain of paper people and decorate it to look like their friends. Talk about how good it is being friends. Talk about what things make it hard to be friends.

Other ideas...

Pretend

Pretend to do impossible things like flying or being invisible. Talk about whether you could make someone walk or be friends with God.

Chat and play

Through the week talk about things you need—such as things you need to make tea. Talk about things you want—such as what book your child would like to read.

Active

Invite a friend or two round to play some games that require them to play together. It's good to be friends! God wants us to be his friends too.

Out and about

Make pictures with chalk on paving stones or walls. Wash away the pictures with water when you have finished. As you play, tell your child that God wipes our bad things away for good—it's really good that they're never here again!

For loads more ideas of how to "Play it", go to

www.thegoodbook.com/playit

Link: Jesus goes to a town called Capernaum. When he gets there he meets a servant with a message from his boss. His boss is a soldier—a very powerful man!

A powerful man needs help

(Luke 7 v 1-10)

Story:

Here is a man. A very **powerful** man. He says: **"Run"** and everyone **runs!** He says: **"Jump"** and everyone **jumps!** He says: **"Stop"** and everyone **stops!**

But his friend is **ill.** The man says: "Get better!" but his friend is still **ill.**

Who can help him?

The man sends Jesus a message.

"I am a very **powerful** man. I say: **"run"** and everyone **runs!** I say: **"jump"** and everyone **jumps!** I say: **"stop"** and everyone **stops.**

"But my friend is **ill.** I can't make him better. Only you can help him."

Jesus says: "Get better!" and right away, just like that, even though he is far away, the man's friend is completely and totally better!

Wow—Jesus did it! Only God's power can do that!

Pray:

Father God, I am glad that Jesus is so powerful. Thank you for all the times you help me.

Tell it

Big idea: Jesus is more powerful than anyone.

Figures and props

- **A figure or toy** to act as the powerful man.
- **A figure or toy** to be the ill/well friend. There's one in the free download. You'll notice that on one side he looks ill and sad, and on the other he is well and happy. Alternatively you could use a paper-plate mask with a happy face on one side and a sad face on the other.
- **A piece of paper in an envelope.** Write the powerful man's message on the paper.

Using the figure of the ill man, show your child his sad face. When Jesus makes him better, turn him around to show him feeling well at the end.

Read out the message the powerful man sends to Jesus.

Telling the story

- Use a **confident** and **bossy** voice for the powerful man. When you read what he says about his ill friend, make him sound **worried** and **sad**.
- Use a **sad** voice when you say "ill".
- Show with your **voice, face** and **body** how **amazing** the healing is!

Tip

If a play idea doesn't work, don't worry! Follow your child's lead and try something different, or try again another time.

Play it

Playing anyway

Remind your child of the story during the week when they're doing activities that require your help, eg: cutting with scissors or using the oven if you bake together.

Create

Make telephones from plastic or paper cups. Make a hole in the bottom of two cups and thread a piece of string through the holes. Tie a large knot at each end of the string. Jesus didn't need a telephone! His words were strong enough to make the ill man better even though he was very far away.

Other ideas...

Pretend

Play at being people who have power and authority. Eg: police officers, parents, kings, teachers.

Out and about

Go to a play park and play a game of comparison. Who can climb the highest? Who can slide the fastest? Who can run to the tree the quickest?

Active

Play "Simon says". Try including some actions that are impossible (eg: "lick your forehead", or "put your elbow in your ear"). Talk about what the man in the story could and couldn't do.

Messy

Play a game of comparing. Get any items you plan to use ready in advance. You could try these: "Are cotton-wool balls or sandpaper softer?" "Is dried spaghetti or a teaspoon stronger?" "Is ice or a tennis ball colder?" "In the story, who was the most powerful—the powerful man or Jesus?"

For loads more ideas of how to "Play it", go to

www.thegoodbook.com/playit

Link: In our story today Jesus goes for a meal at a Pharisee's house. The Pharisees are people who think they can be friends with God by doing lots and lots of good things. While everyone is eating their food, in comes a lady—she wasn't invited and she is definitely not a Pharisee!

A woman loves Jesus

(Luke 7 v 36-50)

Story:

This lady is **sad.** She has done lots and lots of naughty things. She feels all dirty on the inside. She wants to be **friends** with God.

"I know!" says the lady, "I'll go to Jesus!"

She loves Jesus, so she takes him a very special present.

What beautiful perfume.

The lady **cleans** Jesus' dirty feet. He smells lovely now!

"Thank you for **cleaning** my dirty feet," says Jesus. "I can **clean** your dirty heart! I can make you **friends** with God! I'm glad you came to see me!"

The **sad** lady isn't sad anymore! She goes home feeling very **happy!**

Pray:

Thank you God that you want us to be your friends. Thank you that you can make our hearts clean.

Tell it

Big idea: Jesus can make us clean. Jesus can make us friends with God.

Figures and props

- **Bare feet**
- **Liquid soap** or **perfume**
- **A damp cloth**
- **A "smelly bottle"**—see craft opposite.
- **Sad/happy lady**—see the download for a figure you can use, or make a face from a paper plate with a sad face on one side and a happy face on the other.

Use your props to clean your child's feet as you tell the story. Alternatively, try using a picture of Jesus from the free download. Laminate it or cover it in sticky tape. Make Jesus' feet look dirty by colouring on the plastic with a dry-wipe marker or some water-soluble paint. Wipe off the dirt with the cloth as you tell the story.

Encourage your child to experience the beautiful perfume (the "smelly bottle").

Telling the story

- Make a **sad** face when you talk about the lady. Look **disgusted** when you talk about her being dirty on the inside.
- Show a **happy** face and excitement when Jesus talks to the woman. Have a little **cheer** at the end of this **happy** story!

Play it

Create

Make a "smelly bottle" together, or make a few in advance for younger children to explore. Clean out a bottle that has a sports cap. Put something that smells nice inside: try cotton wool/cotton balls with a few drops of essential oils or perfume, or see the free download for more ideas.

Out and about

Collect petals and leaves from flowers and mush them into your very own perfume.

Other ideas...

Messy

Make the inside of a clear plastic bottle "dirty" with some paint and close the lid. Make the outside dirty too. Let your child clean the outside and then help them to see that the inside needs to be made clean as well.

Pretend

Pretend to be cleaning up—allow your child to have a water spray and cloth. Or give a doll a bath.

Active

Play a game of "dodge the hose" where your child has to try to stay dry while you try to get them wet with a hose or a water spray. Do this indoors with bubbles if the weather is bad, or just wrap up warm and use an umbrella.

Playing anyway

Gather rocks or coins and clean them in a bowl of soapy water.

For loads more ideas of how to "Play it", go to

www. thegoodbook .com/playit

A storm stops

(Luke 8 v 22-25)

Link: When Jesus talks, amazing things happen! When Jesus talks, people hear about God. When Jesus talks, ill people are made better. When Jesus talks, people are forgiven—they are friends with God! I wonder what amazing thing will happen when Jesus talks today?

Story:

Jesus and his friends are in a boat. Jesus is **asleep.**

Oh oh! A storm!

The wind is **blowing.** The waves are **splashing.** The boat is **rocking.** But Jesus is **asleep.**

"Help us, Jesus!" his scared friends say.

"The wind is **blowing!** The waves are **splashing!** The boat is **rocking!**"

But Jesus is **asleep.**

Jesus' scared friends call out as loudly as they can: "HELP US, JESUS!!!"

Jesus wakes up.

Jesus hears the wind **blowing.** Jesus sees the waves **splashing.** Jesus feels the boat **rocking.**

What will Jesus do?

"Stop it," says Jesus.

Right that second, just like that, the wind **stops blowing,** the waves **stop splashing** and the boat **stops rocking.**

Everything is **quiet.**

"Wow," say Jesus' scared friends. "Even the wind and the waves do what you say."

Pray:

Father God sometimes I am worried about ....
Sometimes I get scared when .... Please help me to remember that you are strong.

Big idea: Jesus is powerful! He is even in charge of the weather and the water.

Figures and props

- **A toy boat** or an empty plastic tub.
- **A blue sheet or piece of fabric** to act as the lake. Or you could use a container full of water! (Try to take a picture of these, or keep them somewhere safe to use on page 34.)
- **A fan** or **a hairdryer**

Use the fan or hairdryer when you talk about the wind. Use the different speed-settings to make the wind stronger and stronger. Or make whooshing noises with your mouth and blow at each other.

Shake the cloth and let the waves get bigger and bigger.

Rock your body and the boat as you talk about the rocking produced by the storm.

When Jesus says: "Stop it", immediately stop all the noise and movement. Encourage your child to be as still as possible.

22

Play it

Telling the story

- Use your **voice** to express the growing power of the storm—get **louder** and **louder**, and make the scared friends' cries for help sound more desperate. Encourage your child to join in calling for help.
- When Jesus says: **"Stop it"**, pause to show the difference between the **noisy** storm and the **calm** water. Then speak in a **quiet** and **calm** voice.
- In the passage from Luke, the disciples are **terrified** by the power Jesus has shown! So as you finish the story, speak with a tone of **awe** rather than **excitement**.

Other ideas...

Pretend

Pretend you are in a boat during a storm. Use the props from the story, or add some more—shake a bottle or snack tube filled with rice; rustle tin foil; flick a flash light on and off. Pick someone to be in charge—make as much noise as possible until they say: "Stop!".

Out and about

Play a fun game of telling the weather to change, and see if you're as powerful as Jesus!

Active

When you listen to music or dance or play instruments, practise calling out: "Stop!" and getting everyone to freeze!

Create

Make your own symbols for the weather (a sun, raindrops, etc). There's a template in the free download. Use these symbols each day to predict the weather, or to show what weather you would like to have. Even though we know some things about the weather, we're not in charge of it!

For loads more ideas of how to "Play it", go to

www.thegoodbook.com/playit

Messy

Make boats out of old food tubs. Stick in a mast using a straw and modelling clay, and design a paper sail.

WHOOO

Playing anyway

Make a den that feels cosy and secure. Talk about the ideas from the story, such as "safe" and "scared", and how the disciples felt.

Play with your boats in water. Create storms by blowing at the boats through straws, and create rain with water sprays.

Splish! Splash!

Link: People are starting to hear about Jesus. They hear he can make ill people better and they all want to see him. Today Jesus has a big crowd of people around him. There's someone in the crowd who believes Jesus can make her illness better.

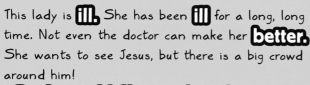

A very ill lady
(Luke 8 v 40-48)

Story:

This lady is **ill.** She has been **ill** for a long, long time. Not even the doctor can make her **better.** She wants to see Jesus, but there is a big crowd around him!

Push, push! Shove, shove! There are so many people **pushing** and **shoving,** the **ill** lady can hardly see Jesus.

So the lady **sque-e-ezes** through the crowds and **re-e-eaches** out her hand and touches Jesus' clothes.

Right away, just like that, the lady is completely and totally **better!**

"Who touched me?" says Jesus.

The crowd stops pushing and shoving.

"Who touched me?" says Jesus.

"It was me!" says the lady. "You made me **better!"**

"I'm glad you believe in me!" says happy Jesus. "You believed in me and so you are **better!"**

Pray:
Jesus, you are amazing. Please help me to believe in you.

Tell it

Big idea: We can believe that Jesus is boss over illness.

Figures and props

- **Illustration or figures** to act as the crowd.
- **A figure or toy** to act as Jesus.
- **Some fabric** such as a tea/hand towel or piece of clothing to act as Jesus' clothing.

Show Jesus almost hidden by the crowd.

As you tell the story, let your child reach out and touch the fabric like the lady did when she touched Jesus' clothing.

Telling the story

- This story starts out quite **sad**—the lady is **sad** and **hopeless.** Express this with the tone of your **voice** and by showing a **sad** and **worried** face. The story changes completely when she is **healed**—let this show in your **voice** and **face.**
- Have fun with the sounds of the words in this story—let your child join in as you **sque-e-eze** and **re-e-each.**

Play it

Messy

Play a game of "Stop that water!" Get a collection of sieves, colanders and plastic bottles/yogurt pots with holes punched in them. Encourage your child to see if they can stop the water getting through the holes. In the story, no one except Jesus could stop the lady being ill.

Pretend

Pretend to be doctors and patients. Now and then, pretend to find illnesses or injuries you can't fix. Remind your child of the lady in the story.

Other ideas...

Create

Make the 'boss' puzzles from the free download. In each one, match the 'boss' with the right picture.

Out and about

Visit a very busy place and play a noticing game. Ask your child to tell you one thing they can: hear; feel with their body; see; smell; and one colour they can spot. Imagine how it must have felt to be in the crowd in the story. You could try telling it "off the cuff" while you're in the busy place.

Playing anyway

Try to use the word "believe" regularly when you are playing. "Have you washed your hands? I believe you." "Do you believe I can win this race?"

Active

Hide some treats around your house, garden or yard and give your child clues to find them. The clues could be spoken or you could draw a map for your child to follow. Talk about how your child believed they would get a treat and they searched until they found it.

For loads more ideas of how to "Play it", go to

www.thegoodbook.com/playit

Link: Do you remember the great big crowd around Jesus? There is someone else in that crowd who wants Jesus to help. His name is Jairus.

A girl who dies

(Luke 8 v 40-56)

Story:

"Help, Jesus!" says a man called Jairus. "My little girl is **ill.**"

"I will help your little girl," Jesus says.

But the crowd is so big and Jesus is so busy, Jairus has to **wait...** and **wait...** and **WAIT!**

Some friends come to Jairus. "It's too late. You **waited** too long. Your little girl is **dead.**"

"Don't be scared," Jesus says to Jairus. "Believe in me. I will help your little girl."

At Jairus' house everyone is **sad.** Jesus goes to the **dead** girl and says: **"Get up,** little girl!"

Right away, just like that, the little girl is **alive!**

"Wow!" says Jairus.

Pray:

Father God, thank you very much that you help us and care for us. Help me to believe in you.

Tell it

Big idea: We can believe Jesus is boss over death.

Figures and props

- **A figure or toy** to act as Jesus.
- **Figures or illustration** to act as the crowd.
- **A figure** to act as Jairus.
- **A figure** to act as Jairus' little girl.

Use the figures to help act out your story as you tell it. Lie the little girl down and stand her up when Jesus brings her back to life.

Telling the story

- As you say: **"Wait"**, use **pauses** and **stretch** out the word to make your child feel like they are having to wait too.
- Show with your **voice** and **facial expressions** how amazing Jesus' miracle is—encourage your child to join in and say: **"Wow"** too!

Tip

Most pre-schoolers are too young to understand what death means. In general, they will struggle to understand the forever-ness of death, and will assume that when people die they come back to life again. So they may not be that amazed by this story (or the story of Jesus' resurrection). This is right for your child's developmental stage, so there is no need to push it if they're not understanding perfectly. This is a happy story, so avoid getting too gloomy!

Play it

Create

Make some cookies together. Cook just a little of the dough—when the timer goes, pretend to be too busy to get the cookies from the oven. Leave them until they are overdone and ruined. Talk about how you waited too long and can't make them better now. Use the rest of the dough to make tasty cookies. Talk about how everyone thought Jesus was too late to help.

Out and about

Play some games against the clock. For example, run to the next lamp post while you count to ten, or find five leaves in 20 seconds. Remind your child of the story—it seemed that Jesus ran out of time, but he still helped Jairus' little girl.

Other ideas...

Pretend

Pretend to be asleep and get your child to try to wake you up—snore loudly and wake up with a yell and a snort!

Messy

Use the idea of something that stops working and won't start again to talk about death. Sort through your dried-up colouring pens or try adding water to old play dough!

Playing anyway

When your child is stuck while they play a game or do an activity, use words from the story such as "wait" and "I will help you".

Active

Play a trust game. Blindfold your child and lead them around an obstacle course. Talk them through it and hold their hand to avoid any trips. Give lots of praise as they go. Talk about how they felt and how it feels to believe what someone says.

For loads more ideas of how to "Play it", go to

www. thegoodbook .com/playit

Jesus feeds lots of people
(Luke 9 v 10-17)

Story:

Look at all these people! Can you count them all?!

Their **tummies** are rumbling—they're hungry.

Jesus' friends have one, two fish and one, two, three, four, five loaves of bread.

Will that be enough for everyone?

Do you think they will need more?

Jesus says: "Thank you for this food, God".

Jesus' friends **give** all the people some bread and some fish to **eat.**

Their **tummies** are full up!

Everyone has had enough!

No one needs more!

Jesus' friends put the leftovers in baskets. Can you count them?

Wow, Jesus—you are amazing!

Pray:

Say some "wow" prayers: "Wow Jesus, you made lots of food out of just a tiny bit!" "Wow God— you really look after people" "Wow Jesus, you are very powerful!"

Tell it

Big idea: Jesus is powerful. He can make a tiny bit of food fill everyone.

Figures and props

- **Two fish shapes** cut from cardboard or paper.
- **Five bits of bread**—it's up to you whether you use five chunks, slices, rolls, etc.
- **Illustration** of the crowd and 12 baskets of leftovers from the free download.

Try counting the people in the picture—make a show of not being able to count them all.

Show your props as you tell the story. Encourage your child to count the bread, fish and baskets with you. Let your child explore them with their hands (and mouth!).

Play it

Telling the story

- To help your child see that there are lots of people and a very small amount of food, use your **tone of voice,** and your **face** and **arms**, to express just how many people there are— sound **tired** just trying to count them! Then use a **smaller voice** and make your body movements much **smaller** when you talk about the tiny amount of food they have. When you talk about how everyone has enough and describe the leftovers, go back to a **bigger voice** and **bigger** movements.

- When you read the questions, use plenty of **expression.** Allow time for your child to think about the question and, if they want to, answer out loud.

Other ideas...

Pretend

Have a picnic (pretend or real!) and re-enact the story.

Chat and play

During meal and snack times, talk about being hungry and being full. Or make a meal together and invite some friends over.

Playing anyway

When you play games that require sharing, talk about whether everyone has enough. Eg: when dealing out cards or sharing marbles or cars.

Active

Do a race where the winner is the first to fill a container. Begin with one large container full of whatever item you are using (balls, toy cars or even water!). Each person must collect one object at a time and bring it back to their own container. Talk about empty and full.

For loads more ideas of how to "Play it", go to

www. thegoodbook .com/playit

Out and about

Go and feed the ducks (or more exotic creatures if you can!). See if you can make sure each duck gets some food.

Qua
Q

Quack!
Quack!

Qu

Can you feed them until they've had enough? Help your child see that the food you brought with you isn't enough to fill them up—you would need more and more!

Messy

Gather together containers of different sizes and spend time pouring water into them to fill them up. You could use jugs of water tinted with food colouring.

Use this water-play to introduce the ideas of empty and full, and enough and too much.

FULL!

EMPTY!

Quack!

Peter starts to see
(Luke 9 v 18-27)

Link: Jesus and his friends are away from all the crowds. Jesus has a question...

Story:

"Who do the crowds think I am?" Jesus asks his friends.

They **remember** all the things Jesus has done. They **remember** all the things Jesus has said.

"They think you're someone special from God," they answer.

"Who do you think I am?" Jesus asks his friends.

They **remember** all the things Jesus has done. They **remember** all the things Jesus has said.

"You are God's **King**," says Peter. "You are **God to the rescue!**"

Who do *you* think Jesus is?

Pray:

God, it is so good that Jesus is our rescuer. Thank you.

Tell it

Big idea: Jesus wants us to know who he is. We know he is God's rescuing King because of all the things he has done and said.

Figures and props

- **Some of the props you used in previous stories,** eg: the net and fish, some bandaged toys, the boat and blue cloth. If you feel these may distract or confuse your child, you could use photos of them instead.

The props should be used to help your child go through the same processes as the disciples as they remember the things they've learned about Jesus. You may want to pause when you say: "They remember all the things Jesus has done", and help your child go through the props and remember.

Telling the story

- As you tell this story, allow **pauses** for your child to think and respond. Use a **questioning tone** of voice.
- Peter's statement about Jesus is really **wonderful!** Say it with real **enthusiasm**— he's just realised Jesus is **God's King!** Things are beginning to click!
- It's OK if your child doesn't want to answer the closing question, but don't be afraid to ask it even as a rhetorical question. Raising questions like this helps our children see that what they think of Jesus matters. It gives them something to chew over in their minds even if they never say anything out loud!

Play it

Chat and play

Enjoy chatting about happy times your child can remember. Make a poster or scrap book from photos.

Create

Make a superhero cape by cutting the arms and front off an old t-shirt. Your child can decorate the neck band and back panel. Be vigilant when your child is wearing it (as with any item that goes round their neck). You could snip the neck band and add a velcro fastener, or safety-pin the cape to the shoulders of their clothing.

Other ideas...

Out and about

On the way to your destination, stop and notice different landmarks (such as traffic lights, a green gate, etc.). On your way home, encourage your child to remember them and point them out, or use them to lead the way home.

Active

Hide a cardboard crown and give your child a time-limit to find it. When they do, shout: "Hooray! You are the King/Queen!"

Pretend

Play a guessing game where you pretend to be different animals or characters. Give clues like: "I stop fires and I wear a helmet" (a firefighter).

Messy

Hide some (cleanable!) toys in different substances and encourage your child to rescue them. Say your child's name: "...... to the rescue!" Try: rummaging through shredded paper, freezing a toy in ice, scooping toys out of a bowl of water. See the free download for more ideas.

For loads more ideas of how to "Play it", go to

www.thegoodbook.com/playit

Link: Do you like hearing stories? Did you know Jesus told stories? Let's listen to a story he told about a wonderful party!

Party time!
(Luke 15 v 1-32)

Story:

Everyone at the party looks very happy! Shall we find out why?

(Man with sheep) Why are you so **happy?**

"I lost one of my sheep. I **looked** and **looked** and I found it—it's safe with me now!" **Hooray!**

(Lady with coin) Why are you so **happy?**

"I lost one of my precious coins. I **looked** and **looked** and didn't give up. I found it—it's safe with me now!" **Hooray!**

(Daddy with son) Why are you so **happy?**

"I lost my son. I **looked** and **looked** and he came back to me. He is safe with me now!" **Hooray!**

Jesus says: "There are wonderful **parties** in heaven when people are safe with God! God is so **happy** when we are safe with him!"

Pray:
God, you must love us so much. Thank you that we can be safe with you.

Tell it

Big idea: Jesus came to make lost people safe. God is so happy when we are found safe with him.

Figures and props
- **Illustrations** of a man with a sheep, a lady with a coin, and a man and his son from the free download.
- Or use **toys** to act as the characters, including a little sheep toy or some cotton wool/cotton balls stuck to a cut-out shape.
- **A coin**
- Things for a party such as **hats, streamers, balloons** and **blowers.**

Telling the story
- The main idea of this story is to show how **glad** God is when we are **safe** with him. When you're telling the parts of the story about the lost sheep, coin and son, look **worried** and **sad.** Then show a **huge difference** in your **tone of voice** and **expressions** when you talk about the lost things being found safe. There can be lots of **cheering** and **smiling** in this story!

Play it

Messy

Use play dough to create party food (a simple recipe can be found in the free download). Use a muffin pan to make pretend cupcakes; create lollies or popsicles by using sticks; cut out cookie shapes; scoop it into bowls for ice cream. Make it look really fancy with sprinkles, glitter, marbles, etc.

Create

Make a treasure box as a safe place for your child's favourite things. Paint an old cardboard container and stick on sparkly sequins, glitter and colourful paper.

Other ideas...

Active

Play hide and seek! Or make a den and use it as a safe base when you play tag. If you're in the safe place, you can't be tagged.

Create

Make a snug house for a favourite cuddly toy. Talk about the people and things that help us feel safe.

Chat and play

Chat about how it feels to lose something precious and how it feels to know our precious things are safe. We must be *very* precious to God! Jesus has made sure we can be safe with God.

Out and about

Prepare a treasure hunt. This can be as simple or convoluted as you like! Set a trail of chalk arrows for your child to follow or give clues. Have plenty of celebrations at the end—try getting hold of some chocolate coins and imagine how happy the woman who found her coin was!

For loads more ideas of how to "Play it", go to

www. thegoodbook .com/playit

Mr. High and Mr. Low
(Luke 18 v 9-14)

Story:

Look at these two men. Here is Mr. **High** and here is Mr. **Low.**

I wonder which man is **friends** with God? Let's listen to them pray.

Mr. **High** says:

"Wow, God! Thank you that I am so brilliant. I do so many good things! I don't do naughty things. I'm glad I'm not like that horrid, naughty Mr. **Low.**"

Mr. **Low** says:

"Oh God, please help me. I am naughty. I need you."

What do you think? Which man is **friends** with God?

Jesus says that Mr. **Low** is God's **friend!**

Pray:

Please help us to remember that we need you. Thank you that we don't have to be brilliant all the time to be your friends.

Tell it

Big idea: Being proud doesn't make us the best, and being good doesn't make us friends with God.

Figures and props

- **Two figures** or toys to act as the men.
- **A high and low platform** for the figures to stand on (eg: a **tower of bricks** or a **pile of books**).

Draw your child's attention to the different figures as each character prays. Encourage your child to point to the person they think is friends with God.

Telling the story

- As you tell this story, **accentuate** the difference between the two men. For Mr. High, sit or stand very **straight** and **tall**, talk in a **confident, smug voice**, and sneer at Mr. Low. For Mr. Low, speak **quietly**, make your body **smaller** by hunching your shoulders and lowering your head, and look **serious** and **sorrowful**.
- Jesus tells this story to **surprise** the listeners—they're used to thinking that the Pharisees are close friends with God. As you finish the story, use a **surprised voice**.

Play it

Pretend

Dress up as athletes for the day (the sillier the better!). Do challenges that have surprising winners: Who can bite their cracker into the most interesting shape? Who can undo a puzzle and get it back in its box the fastest? There are lots more ideas in the free download. Give out prizes for everyone.

Messy

Make salt-dough medals and decorate them (see the free download for a recipe). Wear these in your games through the week.

Other ideas...

Active

Play high-jump and limbo. It's easy for the biggest person to jump the highest but the smallest person can get the lowest.

Create

Set up a mending station where you can fix favourite toys and books that have been broken. Tape together torn pages, glue on a car's broken wheels, sew up a stuffed toy. Talk about how much you love these things even though they aren't the strongest, prettiest or the best.

Chat and play

Take opportunities this week to show your child that you're quick to say sorry to God and to them.

Playing anyway

Build towers of different heights with bricks and see which one falls over most easily. The tall tower looks impressive but the small tower stays standing.

For loads more ideas of how to "Play it", go to

www.thegoodbook.com/playit

Link: Jesus is walking through a town called Jericho. He is on his way to the big city of Jerusalem. There is a man in Jericho who wants to know Jesus. I wonder if Jesus will want to know him?

Zacchaeus
(Luke 19 v 1-10)

Story:

This is Zacchaeus. Zacchaeus takes people's money and keeps it for himself. Zacchaeus makes people **sad** and cross. No one wants to be his **friend.** No one ever wants to go to his house for **dinner.**

Can you spot Zacchaeus now? There he is! Up a tree!

"Hello Zacchaeus," Jesus says. "I'm coming to your house for **dinner."**

What a surprise! Jesus wants to be Zacchaeus' **friend!**

Jesus has made Zacchaeus very **happy.** "I will give back everything I've taken from people and will give them even more," he says.

Now Zacchaeus is **friends** with Jesus, everything has changed!

Pray:
Wow Jesus! It's so good to be friends with you!

Tell it

Big idea: Being friends with Jesus changes everything.

Figures and props
- **A figure or toy** to act as Zacchaeus.
- **Some people**
- **A tower of blocks** to act as a tree. (You could use brown and green blocks or put them next to a picture of a tree to make it seem more tree-like!)
- **A figure or toy** to act as Jesus.
- **Coins** or **a piggy bank.**

Begin with half the money next to the people; then move it to Zacchaeus when you say he takes their money.

When you say that no one wants to be Zacchaeus' friend, move the people away from him.

Put Zacchaeus on the blocks as though he's climbing a tree.

Put Jesus and Zacchaeus close together, and then move the money back to the people. Have some extra coins to one side and show Zacchaeus giving back even more than he took.

Play it

Telling the story

- Begin with a tone that makes it clear that people think Zacchaeus is really **nasty.** Sound **shocked** as you describe the **selfish** things he does.
- Change tone when Jesus speaks—show that he's **not cross** or **disapproving.**

- **Gasp** when you say: **"What a surprise!"** and encourage your child to join in. Show **happiness** and **amazement** as you describe the **change** in Zacchaeus.

Other ideas...

Pretend

Play shops and use real or pretend money to buy and sell. Get familiar with the concepts of give and take. This may raise other themes from the story like fairness, taking what belongs to someone else, and being generous.

Active

Climb a tree or climbing frame/jungle gym to help you remember the story together. What can you see when you're up high?

Playing anyway

Play a game of snap and talk about taking and giving. It can look like one person is winning, and then everything changes! If your child gets upset when they lose cards, talk about how the people felt when Zaccheaus took their things.

Messy

Create ice blocks of different sizes and colours and talk about the changes you see as they melt. See what things make them melt faster (eg: putting it in a bowl of water, holding it in your hands, adding salt, covering it with a woolly hat).

For loads more ideas of how to "Play it", go to

www.thegoodbook.com/playit

Create

Make a butterfly picture with a piece of paper folded in half. Draw a caterpillar along the central crease. On one side of the paper, paint a butterfly wing; then fold the paper over and press down.

Open it out and see your butterfly emerge! Talk about the big change of a caterpillar becoming a butterfly.

Out and about

Do a carwash for any trikes, bikes or scooters your child has. Take a before and after picture, and notice the big change!

Scrub! Scrub!

A meal with Jesus
(Luke 22 v 7-23)

Story:

Jesus and his friends are having their special Passover meal.

Jesus shares some drink and some bread with his friends.

"Very soon I will be taken away and hurt," says Jesus. "This is the last thing I will **eat** or **drink** before I die."

"When you **eat** and **drink** together, **remember** me."

Jesus' friends feel **sad** and scared. I wonder what will happen next?

 Tip Try doing this story at a meal or snack time.

Pray:
Help us to remember you, Jesus. Help us to remember that you are good, even when things are sad and scary.

Tell it

Big idea: Being friends with Jesus changes everything.

Figures and props

- **A figure or toy** to act as Jesus.
- **Some figures or toys** to act as the disciples.
- **A drink**
- **Some bread**

Share the drink and bread as you tell the story.

Telling the story

- This story could cause some children to feel worried. To try to maintain the tone of the story without being unduly frightening, keep your voice **quiet** and don't rush through the story.
- Look **sad** and **scared** when you talk about the disciples' feelings. It's ok if your child feels like

the disciples did—offer plenty of **cuddles** and **reassurance** if they are feeling **worried**.

 Tip

The next three stories talk about serious things which could be unsettling for your child. Try to offer plenty of space for your child to chat about what they're learning, especially if they haven't thought about death before. Don't feel you have to keep the resurrection as a surprise—it's good for our children to know these sad stories have a happy ending.

Play it

Out and about

On a walk, pick up mementoes of your journey and make a collage with them when you get home.

Pretend

Have fun imagining some special meals—pretend it is a birthday meal or Christmas dinner. Think of all the delicious food you will eat and imagine all the people you would want to share it with. Use play food to help you act out your special meal.

Other ideas...

Messy

Make gloop together (two parts cornflour/cornstarch to one part water). Ask your child what they think will happen if they mix the water and cornflour. Will it be hard or soft? Will it pour like water or be squashy like dough? Allow your child to experiment with the ingredients. Keep asking: "I wonder what will happen next?"

Active

Do a dance-move challenge! Show your child a dance move and ask them to remember it and do it back to you. Make the game harder by putting lots of moves together. Let your child challenge you too. Talk about Jesus asking his friends to remember.

Chat and play

Every time you eat bread this week, take the chance to say: "Oh! Do you remember our story?"

Playing anyway

Play memory games such as pairs or Kim's game. Use words from the story as you play: "Can you remember?" and "What will happen next?"

For loads more ideas of how to "Play it", go to

www.thegoodbook.com/playit

Jesus is taken away and put on trial

(Luke 22 v 54-71)

Link: While Jesus is in Jerusalem, lots of people are glad to see him, but some important people don't like Jesus at all. They want to stop him.

Story:

The angry crowd take Jesus to important men who don't like him at all. They want to  Jesus. They want to get rid of Jesus. They want to kill Jesus so he will be gone for ever.

The important men ask Jesus questions:

"Are you God's **King?**" they ask.

"Are you God's **Son?**" they say.

"**Yes,**" says Jesus.

The important men and the angry crowd get angrier and angrier. They don't want Jesus to be their They want to kill Jesus so he will be gone for ever.

Pray:

Thank you Jesus that you are God's King. Thank you Jesus that you are God's Son.

Tell it

Big idea: Jesus is God's Son, the King. The people don't want Jesus to be their King.

Figures and props

- **Illustration** of the angry crowd and important men from the free download. Alternatively, use **figures or toys** to act as these characters.
- **A figure or toy** to act as Jesus.

As you tell the story, act out the angry crowd coming for Jesus and taking him to the important men. As you say: "Stop", lift and tap your Jesus figure back down. As you say: "Get rid", move Jesus away. As you say: "Kill", make Jesus lie down. When you say: "They don't want Jesus to be their King", turn the crowd and important men so they have their backs to Jesus.

Telling the story

- When you talk about the crowd and important men being **angry,** use a **grumpy-sounding voice** (avoid sounding **too angry,** especially if it will make your child feel **worried**).
- Ask the important men's questions in a **disbelieving** voice and speak **confidently** when you say: **"Yes"** in reply.

Play it

Themes: Getting rid of things. Gone. What it means for Jesus to be King and God's Son. What it means to not want Jesus as King. Plus general play to help your child remember and talk about the story.

Active

Wear crowns and play a game of tag—the object of the game is to take each other's crown away. Say: "I don't want you to be King", as you grab the crown!

Messy

Set up a taste-testing station and get your child to taste a variety of foods. For each one they decide whether they like it or don't like it, and whether they want to keep it or get rid of it.

Other ideas...

Pretend

Play at being kings, queens or someone in charge, like a teacher. Imagine what a good ruler would do (be kind, make good decisions for the subjects, etc). Then imagine what a bad ruler would do (be mean, boss everyone around, etc). Act out being both. Ask your child what sort of King they think Jesus is.

Chat and play

Get your child to help you as you take the bins or garbage cans out. Talk about how the people wanted to get rid of Jesus just as we get rid of refuse.

Playing anyway

Read fairy tales together and spot the good and bad rulers.

Create

Make footprint pictures using bare feet or welly/rain boots. Use them to talk about having Jesus as our King. If we want him as our King, we follow him (show all the footprint pictures going in the same direction). If we don't want him as our King, we go our own way (show some footprint pictures turning the other way).

For loads more ideas of how to "Play it", go to

www.thegoodbook.com/playit

Link: Today's story is a sad one—people want to stop Jesus. Let's think about some of the great things we know about Jesus. I don't think they'll be able to stop Jesus for ever!

Jesus dies
(Luke 23 v 26-53)

Story:

Jesus' **hands** can make hurt people better.

But today his **hands** get hurt when the angry crowd put him on a cross.

Jesus' **voice** can stop a storm.

But today his **voice** says: "God, my Daddy, forgive them".

Jesus' friends **see** he hasn't done anything wrong.

But today Jesus' friends **see** that he dies.

Jesus' friends put him in a tomb. They feel so **sad.** They think he is gone for ever. They don't know that soon they will feel his **hands** again, soon they will hear his **voice** again, soon they will **see** he is alive again. **"Goodbye** Jesus," say his sad friends.

Pray:

Jesus, you are so strong and so good. You died and we can be friends with God. You are wonderful.

Tell it

Big idea: Jesus is strong, powerful and good but dies like someone who is weak, small and bad.

Figures and props

- **Wooden blocks** in the shape of a cross with a block in front for Jesus to stand on.
- **A figure or toy** to act as Jesus.
- **A tomb.** You could use anything for this (**a bag,** an old **ice-cream tub**), or you could make one in the craft suggested opposite.

Telling the story

- This is a **sad** story. Speak in a **gentle** way and tell the story **slowly**.
- Use your face to express Jesus' **pain** when his hands are hurt and to show the **sadness** of his friends when he dies.
- Emphasise the repeated words: **"hands"**, **"voice"** and **"see"**.
- Jesus dies: it is a **shock**; it is sad; but it is **not** for ever.

Tip

Very small children will struggle to grasp concepts like "for ever", and that death means not breathing or eating or doing anything that alive people do. Don't be concerned if your child seems a little confused or if they appear to think that everyone who dies will come right back—it's a very normal reflection of their developmental stage!

Play it

Create

Make a tomb by scrunching foil into a cave shape and scrunching another piece of foil into a ball to act as the stone covering the tomb. Make it large enough to fit the figure you have been using to show Jesus. Leave your tomb as it is or paint it with a mixture of white glue and poster paint.

Messy

Plant seeds on damp cotton wool/cotton balls, or in soil/compost in empty yogurt pots. Keep watering and watching to see what happens. Talk about how small and useless the seeds look.

Other ideas...

Active

Play hide and seek, or take it in turns to hide a toy for the other person to find. Talk about how Jesus was hidden and that his friends thought they would never see him again.

Chat and play

Talk about Jesus' friends—what they knew about Jesus and how they felt when he died. It's sad to say goodbye when we love someone.

Out and about

Gather some plants and flowers (or get some from a florist), and put them in a vase without water. Notice the change in the plants as they die.

Pretend

Pretend to be getting ready for a party and ask your child to help you wrap a present. This will eventually be a gift that your child gets to keep, so choose something that will be a real pleasure for them to receive. Put the present somewhere where your child can see it but not get hold of it.

For loads more ideas of how to "Play it", go to

www.thegoodbook.com/playit

Link: Do you remember the last story we did? Jesus died on the cross. Do you think his friends are feeling happy or sad?

Jesus is alive!

(Luke 24 v 1-43)

Story:

Here is one of Jesus' friends.

How do you feel? Are you **sad?**

"I feel **happy!** I went to the tomb and what a surprise! Angels told me Jesus is **alive!"**

Here are two of Jesus' friends.

How do you feel—are you **sad?**

"No, we're not **sad!** We are **happy!**

"We went on a long walk and we saw Jesus! He is **alive!"**

Jesus' friends are all together. I wonder how they feel? Do you feel **sad?**

"We are **happy!**

"Look—Jesus is with us! He was dead and now he is **alive!"**

What a wonderful day!

Pray:

Jesus! You're alive! What happy news!

Tell it

Big idea: We can be happy! Jesus was dead but now he is alive!

Figures and props

- Enough **figures** for all the friends in the story. The first friends to see Jesus in Luke 24 are women, and it is Mary Magdalene who tells the rest of the disciples the good news, so try to have at least one female friend!
- Alternatively you could **draw smiley faces on your fingertips** and use your fingers to act as the friends.
- **A figure or toy** to act as Jesus.
- **A tomb**—use the one you made last week, or an old box or plastic tub.
- **Figures or toys** to act as angels.

Act out the story using the figures. It will be easier if you can get the three different groups of friends set up before you begin.

Telling the story

- When you ask the friends how they feel, sound **concerned** and **inquisitive**—when you say: "sad", make a really **sad** face and use a **sad** voice. In contrast, reply in a really **happy** voice with a really **happy** face!
- This is such a **joyful** story! Build up the **excitement** and **happiness** as you go through—as the numbers of friends increase, let your **enthusiastic** tone increase too!

Play it

Create

Make double-sided masks out of paper plates. On one side have a happy face and on the other have a sad face. Use the masks to talk about things that make your child happy or sad.

Messy

Explore the seeds you sowed last week. Has anything changed? It looked like the seeds were small and useless but they have grown! Plant more seeds—this time choose something that excites your child.

RIIIIIIP!

TEAR!

Other ideas...

Playing anyway

Play with a jack-in-the-box, or play games like *Jenga* and *Buckaroo*, and talk about surprises.

Active

Play sleeping lions or sleepy bunnies (see the free download for instructions). Talk about Jesus being dead and then alive again.

Out and about

Go on a long walk (20 minutes may feel like for ever!). Imagine what it was like for the friends who met Jesus while they were walking. Try getting a friend to meet you on your journey, or imagine you have amazing news and run home to share it!

Pretend

Have a pretend party and give your child the present you set aside (see "Pretend" for the previous story). Talk about how it was hidden in the wrapping paper and now it's back and your child can keep it!

For loads more ideas of how to "Play it", go to

www. thegoodbook .com/playit

Link: No one can stop Jesus! Jesus was dead but now he is alive again!

Time for Jesus to go

(Luke 24 v 44-53)

Story:

Jesus' friends are so **happy** that he is **alive** again!

"It's **time** for me to go now," says Jesus. **"Remember** to tell everyone all about me.

"You won't be on your own—God will be with you. His Spirit will help you all the time."

Thank you God! **Bye bye,** amazing Jesus!

Pray:

Thank you that you are with us all the time. Help us to tell people about you.

Tell it

Big idea: God will always be with us. We can remember what Jesus has done and tell people about him.

Figures and props

- **A figure or toy** to act as Jesus.
- **A figure or toy** to act as Jesus' friends.

Act out the story with your figures.

Telling the story

- It may come as a **shock** to your child that Jesus is going away—they may feel quite **sad** about it. Tell the story in a matter-of-fact and **positive** tone. Talk with **excitement** and **happiness** about the help that God will provide.

Tip

While you play, it may be fun to re-tell the story or ask questions such as: "Does that remind you of our story?" But using the play themes means that even if you don't talk about it, you will be reinforcing the story's message anyway!

Play it

Themes: Remember. Telling. Saying goodbye. Plus general play to help your child remember and talk about the story.

Create

Make a card to share with a friend. Draw pictures of some of the things Jesus has done. Use the card to help your child tell their friend what they know about Jesus—they could even invite their friend along to church or to a group they go to.

Out and about

Go to a nearby river and throw in leaves and twigs. Say: "Goodbye" as they float away.

Other ideas...

Pretend

Play a game of being in a café or going to the shops—see if your child can remember your order or all the items on the shopping list.

Active

Teach your child a simple hand-clapping rhythm to go with a favourite song. See if they can remember it; then see if they can show it to someone else!

Chat and play

If you leave your child in a crêche or nursery, or even when you leave the room, use it as a moment to say: "I'm going, but I'm coming back". When you leave places together, use the words from the story: "It's time to go".

Messy

Look back through the book and pick some messy play ideas that your child has really enjoyed. Do the activities again and see if your child can tell you about the stories they are linked with. Talk about the things you've learned about Jesus.

For loads more ideas of how to "Play it", go to

www. thegoodbook .com/playit

53

Actions

Tip↗

There are lots of actions listed here—do remember these are for you to pick and choose. Don't feel you have to do them all and exhaust yourself! This is especially worth remembering if you're using some of the props for a story—your hands will be busy enough!

Here comes Jesus

King: pretend to place a crown on your head or do a bow.
No: shake head and make a "don't be silly" face.
Yes: nod and smile.
God to the rescue!: raise a fist in the air as though you're flying like a superhero.

Jesus in the desert

Listen(s) / listening: cup your hand behind your ear.
No: shake your head.

Jesus makes lots of people better

Hands: wave your hands and use your hands to touch the toys.
Touches: use a finger to touch your other hand, or touch any toys you're using as props.

So many fish!

Tired: yawn and stretch.
Heave: act as if it's really hard to bring up the full net.

Jesus helps a man who can't walk

Walk(s): make your index and middle fingers walk, or walk on the spot.
Friend(s): hug yourself (or your child!).
Hooray!: hands in the air while you cheer, thumbs up or some other celebratory move!

A powerful man needs help

Powerful: show your muscles!

Run(s)... jump(s)... stop(s): run and jump on the spot; then stand totally still. If you're sitting down for the story, you could use your fingers instead—make your middle and index fingers run, jump and stop.

Ill: thumbs down.

A woman loves Jesus

Sad: show a sad face and point to your sad-looking mouth.

Friends: hug yourself (or your child!).

Clean(s): do an action as though you're cleaning something with your hands or scrubbing your hands clean.

Happy: show a happy face and point to your smiling mouth.

A storm stops

Asleep: put your hands together near one cheek, rest your head on your hands and close your eyes.

Blowing: blow with your mouth.

Splashing: move your hand across your body and trace the shape of waves, getting bigger and bigger.

Rocking: rock your body.

Stop: put your hand up as though stopping traffic.

Quiet: put your index finger on your lips.

A very ill lady

Ill: thumbs down, sad face. **Better:** thumbs up, happy face.

Push: push hands forward.

Shove: act like you're pushing something to the side.

Squeezes: make your body really small as though trying to fit in a tiny gap.

Reaches: stretch out a hand.

A girl who dies

Wait: tap wrist.
Dead / Ill: thumbs down.
Sad: show a sad face and point to your sad-looking mouth.
Get up: raise hands up.
Alive: thumbs up.

Jesus feeds lots of people

Tummies: rub tummy. Look sad or happy depending on whether they are hungry or full up.
Give: act out sharing the food.
Eat: pretend to put food in your mouth.

Peter starts to see

Remember: tap your temple with your index finger.
King: pretend to place a crown on your head or do a bow.
God to the rescue!: raise a fist in the air as though you're flying like a superhero.

Party time!

Happy: show a happy face and point to your smiling mouth.
Looked: shield your eyes with your hand and act out searching.
Hooray!: hands in the air while you cheer, thumbs up or some other celebratory move!
Parties: pretend to dance and celebrate.

Mr. High and Mr. Low

High: thumbs up, hands held high.
Low: thumbs down, hands lower.
Friends: hug yourself (or your child!).

Tip

Try doing the actions for "High" and "Low" when Mr. High and Mr. Low speak. It will help your child know who is talking, and sums up their attitudes as they pray.

Zacchaeus

Sad: show a sad face and point to your sad-looking mouth.
Friend: hug yourself (or your child!).
Dinner: pretend to eat.
Happy: show a happy face and point to your smiling mouth.

A meal with Jesus

Eat: pretend to put food in your mouth.
Drink: pretend to drink.
Remember: tap your temple with your index finger.
Sad: show a sad face and point to your sad-looking mouth.

Jesus is taken away and put on trial

Stop: hand up like you're stopping traffic.
King: pretend to place a crown on your head or do a bow.
Son: Put your hand on your head as though measuring your height, then move it lower and to the side of you as though measuring someone smaller than you.
Yes: nod your head.

Jesus dies

Hands: show hands as you speak.
Voice: point to your mouth with both index fingers.
See: point index fingers at eyes, then move forward away from your face.
Sad: show a sad face and point to your sad-looking mouth.
Goodbye: wave.

Jesus is alive! // Time for Jesus to go

Sad: show a sad face and point to your sad-looking mouth.
Happy: show a happy face and point to your smiling mouth.
Alive: hands either side of face, palms forward, fingers wriggling.
Time: tap wrist with index finger of other hand.
Remember: tap your temple with your index finger.
Bye: wave.

Downloads

Visit our website for downloads

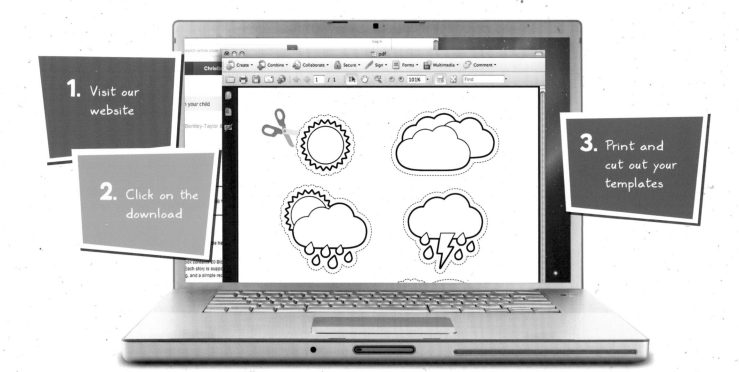

1. Visit our website

2. Click on the download

3. Print and cut out your templates

Templates

On the next three pages you'll find templates for some of the activities in this book. These are also available—plus figures, crowd scenes and pictures to use for storytelling—on our website:

www.thegoodbook.com/playit

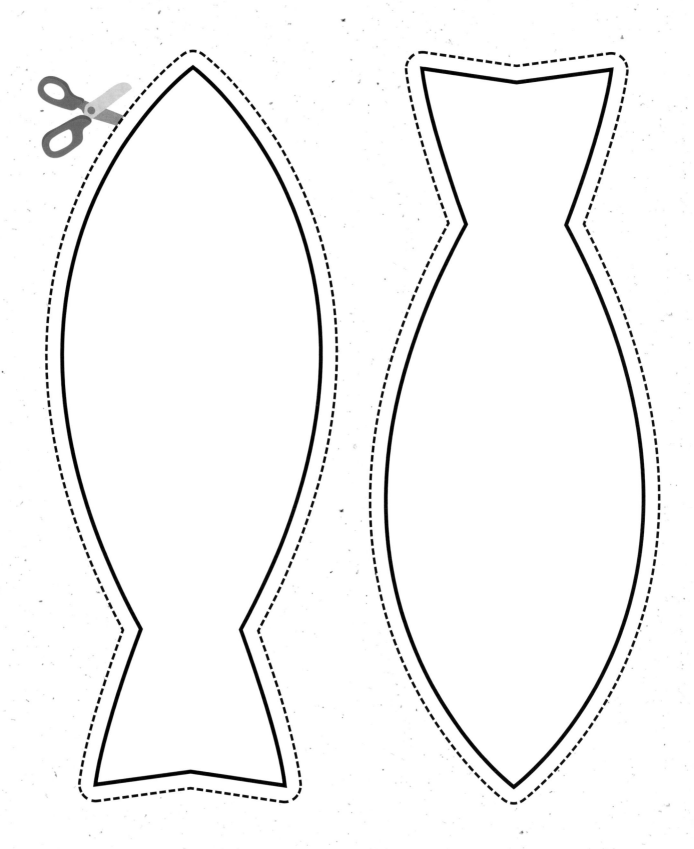

1.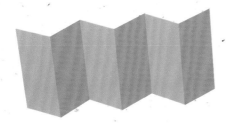

2.

3.

About the author

Alice Buckley lives in Lancashire, England. She is married to Dave and is Mum to Mikey, Dan and Jemima. Alice loves Jesus, drinking tea, writing and reading. Alice writes about messy family life, disability, adoption and faith at www.playontheword.com

Thank you

Tremendous thanks to Dave (oh, your patience!) and our lovely, wild kids. Getting to hang out with you lot is my favourite thing. Mikey, you may never know that you inspired this book but without you it never would have happened.

Thanks to the kind blog readers who urged me to write this book and particular thanks to the Brays, Chaplins, Dyes, Hesslegraves, Keenes, Mckays, Merricks, Rycrofts and Tinkers for their kind feedback.

Thanks to the team at The Good Book Company. Especially to the ever-encouraging Alison, and to André for making it look great.

Bible-reading resources
for children and families

Bake through the Bible

20 fun cooking activities to explore the Bible story with young children.

Beginning with God

Bible-study notes for pre-schoolers with 44 colour stickers. Linked with *The Beginner's Bible* but can be used with any pre-schooler Bible.

XTB

Annual subscription available

Packed with puzzles, pictures, prayers and solid teaching for 7-10s. Twelve issues available.

Table Talk

Annual subscription available

Three months of Bible times to help families discover God's Word together.

www.thegoodbook.com